Japanese Dessert Cookbook

The Most Decadent Japanese Recipes Guide

Including Special Mouthwatering Japanese Desserts

By

Martha Stephenson

Copyright 2016 Martha Stephenson

License Notes

No part of this Book can be reproduced in any form or by any means including print, electronic, scanning or photocopying unless prior permission is granted by the author.

All ideas, suggestions and guidelines mentioned here are written for informative purposes. While the author has taken every possible step to ensure accuracy, all readers are advised to follow information at their own risk. The author cannot be held responsible for personal and/or commercial damages in case of misinterpreting and misunderstanding any part of this Book

Table of Contents

Introduction 5
1. Strawberry Rice Cake 7
2. Three-Ingredient Japanese Cheesecake 10
3. Miso Cookies 13
4. Ice Cream Dorayaki Recipe 15
5. Purin Recipe 18
6. Green Tea (Matcha) Ice Cream 21
7. Coffee Jelly 24
8. Japanese Candied Sweet Potatoes 26
9. Matcha Ganache 28
10. Kabocha Squash Yokan 30
11. Mizu Youkan 32
12. Fruit Jelly 34
13. Castella 36
14. Dango 38
15. Kinako Chestnut 40
16. Matcha Milk Adzuki Bread 42
17. Suama 45
18. Taiyaki 47
19. Yatsuhashi 49
20. Kuzumochi 52
21. Manju 54
22. Coconut Pearl Tapioca with Tropical Fruit 57

23. Japanese Jersey Milk Vanilla Ice-Cream 59
24. Mochi Biscuits 61
25. Karukan 63
26. Kabocha Manju 65
27. Candied Black Beans 67
28. Matcha Green Tea Chia Pudding 69
29. Mochi Ice Cream 71
30. Strawberry Condensed Milk Japanese Shaved Ice 74
Conclusion 76
About the Author 78
Author's Afterthoughts 80

Introduction

Japan is not only famous for pioneering the field of technology but also its vast and exuberant culture. When we talk about culture, the first and foremost part of every culture is its food. Pick any country around the world and you will see how greatly it is defined by its traditional cuisine.

Japanese food is famous all around the world. There are roughly about 106 kinds of Japanese food which include their famous desserts. Long before sugar was so commonly used across the globe, Japan started making desserts from simple ingredients such as rice and sweet beans and from that point onwards the innovation of unique desserts started.

Even today when it comes to Japanese desserts, one cannot not stop but be fascinated by the techniques and ingredients these desserts are made from. Some of the very famous desserts which are also a part of this cookbook are mochi, daifuku, dorayaki, dango, manju and coffee jelly.

This Japanese dessert cookbook features thirty recipes that are popular even outside Japan. The preparation method of each recipe is so detailed that an amateur chef can also execute a complete professional dessert in first attempt. Most ingredients of these desserts are already in your pantry and those which are not; they are easily available at any Asian supermarket.

These Japanese dessert recipes will definitely be a hit among your friends and family. With these vast dessert choices you can now experience the authentic flavors of Japan right in the comfort of your home. The presentation of every dessert is of great value and counts for how tempting it looks so make sure you put extra effort on your presentation skills.

1. Strawberry Rice Cake

Strawberry rice cake also known as ichigo daifuku in Japanese is a traditional strawberry dessert where the juicy strawberries are wrapped with anko and mochi mixture and shaped into decent balls. The sourness of strawberries adds a bold flavor to the overall confection.

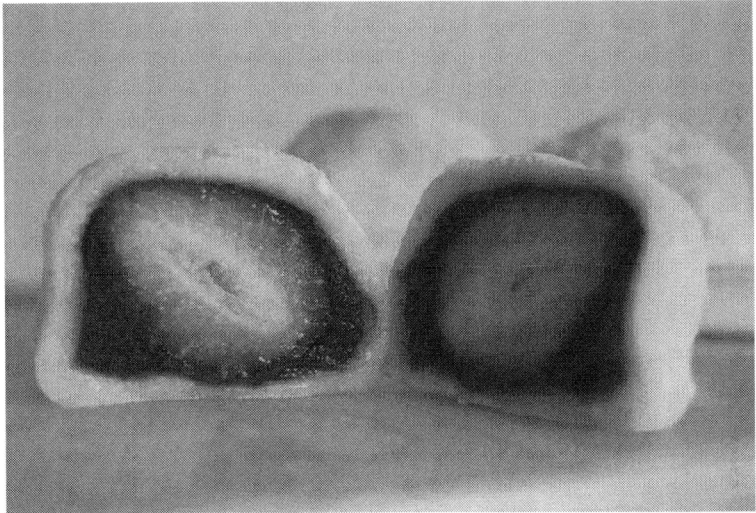

Servings: 6

Preparation time: 20 minutes

Ingredients:

- Glutinous rice flour (mochiko), 5/8 cups
- Strawberries, 5
- Water, 5/8 cups
- Corn starch, for dusting
- Sugar, 2 tablespoons
- Sweet red bean paste (Anko), ¾ cup

Method:

Combine flour and sugar in a bowl and keep aside.

Hull strawberries and arrange on paper tower to pat dry. Keep aside.

Make five anko balls for same size and cloak the strawberries with these balls only leaving the tip unwrapped.

Now add water to the flour mixture gradually and mix using a silicone spatula. Combine until thick. Heat the mixture in the microwave for a minute and mix again. Cover with plastic and microwave for another minute. Mix again with the spatula and cover with plastic and microwave for 30 seconds. The mixture will turn translucent by now.

Dust corn starch over the counter. Take out the flour mixture from the bowl and put it on the dusted counter add some more corn starch on top.

Flatten mochi mixture and fold in half. Divide it into five pieces.

Flatten each piece and place strawberry on it. Carefully wrap the strawberry with mochi and twist the edges to seal tightly.

Let cool for an hour before serving.

2. Three-Ingredient Japanese Cheesecake

This delicate three ingredient cheesecake is super easy to make. The trick is to whip and combine everything well. The perfect consistency of the egg whites is when you whip them and invert the bowl and the mixture doesn't fall off. The other ingredients are added to the chocolate while it is still in the double boiler so be very careful not to overheat it.

Servings: 4

Preparation time: 30 minutes

Ingredients:

- Cream cheese, 120 g
- White chocolate, 120 g
- Eggs, 3

Method:

Crack eggs in a bowl and separate the yolks. Refrigerate the whites for 2 hours or as long as possible.

Preheat the oven to 338 F.

Melt chocolate in a double boiler. Make sure you do not burn it.

Whip chilled whites until soft peaks forms.

Add cream cheese to the melted chocolate and stir to combine.

Now add yolks and combine them well in the chocolate mixture.

Take 1/3 of the whites' mixture and fold it gently in the chocolate mixture. Repeat with the remaining whites, adding 1/3 of it each time.

Combine well and make sure you do not rush in combining the mixture.

Prepare a baking pan with parchment paper and brush it with a little butter. Transfer the mixture to the pan and place the pan over a baking sheet filled with a little hot water.

Bake for 15 minutes then turn the temperature to 320 F and continue baking for another 15 minutes. Now stop the heat and bake for final 15 minutes.

Let the cake cool completely before taking it out of the pan.

Serve

3. Miso Cookies

These round morsels are baked to perfection with a combination of nutty and salty flavor and a perfect crunch that a cookie should have. These cookies will last up to a week provided that you store them in an air tight jar. Enjoy with your evening tea or devour these goodies in the middle of night.

Servings: 3 dozens

Preparation time: 2 hours 20 minutes

Ingredients:

- Miso paste, 2 tablespoons
- All-purpose flour, 1 ½ cup
- Raw sugar
- Butter, ½ cup, at room temperature
- Egg. ½ beaten
- Baking soda, ½ teaspoon
- Sugar, ½ cup

Method:

Combine miso paste, sugar and butter in a bowl and whisk until well combined and creamy.

Add eggs and whisk again.

Now add flour and baking soda and mix until a smooth dough forms.

Divide the dough in half and form 2 inch round logs from each half. Roll them with raw sugar and cover with plastic. Refrigerate for 2 hours.

Preheat oven to 350 F.

Cut dough into thick round pieces and flatten it a bit.

Arrange on a lined cookie sheet and bake for 15 minutes.

Let cool at room temperature before serving.

4. Ice Cream Dorayaki Recipe

Ingredients:

Dorayaki are like a Japanese version of pancakes only a little denser and fluffier. The spongy base of dorayaki is topped with anko giving out a sweet but strong flavor and vanilla ice cream for a complete frozen dessert experience. Make sure you freeze the cakes until the ice cream hardens.

Servings: 6

Preparation time: 1 hour

Ingredients:

- Vanilla ice cream, 1 container

For Dorayaki:

- All-purpose flour, 1 ¼ cup
- Milk, ¾ cup
- Baking soda, 1 teaspoon
- Honey, 1 tablespoon
- Eggs, 2
- Sugar, ½ cup
- Anko

Method:

Combine flour and baking soda in a bowl.

In a large bowl whisk eggs with honey, milk and sugar.

Now make a well in between the flour mixture and slowly pour milk. Combine well and form a smooth batter.

Spray a pan with cooking spray and pour 1/8 cup of batter onto the pan. Cook like you make pancakes. Give each side a cooking time for at least 2 minutes.

Transfer to paper towel.

Slather anko on one cake then a scoop of ice cream and top it with another cake. Repeat with all the cakes and wrap them with plastic.

Freeze them for a few hours.

Enjoy when the ice cream has hardened fully.

5. Purin Recipe

Purin is a Japanese version of flan and is served cold. It is better to leave it overnight in the refrigerator. The texture of this cold dessert is firm and the caramel sauce works as a perfect base. You can top it with whipped cream or berries if you like.

Servings: 8

Preparation time: 45 minutes

Ingredients:

For Custard:

- Milk, 2 cups + 1 tablespoon
- Vanilla extract, 1 teaspoon
- Eggs, 3
- Sugar, ½ cup
- For Caramel Syrup:
- Sugar, 1 cup
- Water, 3 tablespoons

Method:

Combine sugar and water in a pot and heat until the sugar changes its color to dark brown. DO NOT STIR.

Once the sugar dissolves completely, stir once and divide the syrup among eight ramekins. You probably will have some leftover syrup.

For custard, heat milk but do not boil.

Meanwhile whisk eggs with sugar and stir in the milk. Strain milk in a large bowl and add vanilla extract.

Now divide custard among the ramekins.

Arrange ramekins in a baking pan and fill it with a little hot water. Be careful not to splash water on the custard.

Preheat the oven to 350 F and bake the custard for 45 minutes.

Refrigerate for 3 hours at least.

Enjoy.

6. Green Tea (Matcha) Ice Cream

Matcha is the powdered form of green tea and not those leaves that you use in making tea. Green tea powder when combined with milk not only brings out a beautiful green color but also tastes delicious and is perfect for making desserts. Green tea ice cream is a popular choice of ice cream in Japan as well as outside Japan.

Servings: 1 container

Preparation time: 7 hours

Ingredients:

- Green tea powder (matcha), 2 tablespoons
- Sugar, ½ cup + 2 tablespoons
- Milk, 2 cups
- Heavy cream, 1 cup
- Egg yolks, 6

Method:

Pour ice water in a bowl and keep aside.

Whisk ¼ cup milk with tea powder and dissolve the particles completely. Now add this to the remaining milk and whisk again to combine.

Combine ½ cup of cream with milk and heat it until it reaches boiling point. Turn off the heat.

In another bowl whisk yolks with remaining cream and sugar.

Gradually stir milk in the egg mixture and combine.

Return the mixture to heat and stir until it thickens.

Now place the pot in ice water and let it sit there for some time.

Transfer mixture to an ice cream container and refrigerate for three hours.

Now follow the instructions of your ice cream maker. Every brand has a different time set.

Freeze again for another three hours then serve.

7. Coffee Jelly

Coffee jelly is a famous cold dessert in Japan made with strong black coffee. The gelatin helps maintain the jelly-ish texture of this dessert and you can always adjust the sweetness according to your liking. In case you don't have strong coffee available you can also use espresso and add a distinct whiff to your dessert.

Servings: 3

Preparation time: 20 minutes

Ingredients:

- Hot strong coffee, 480 ml
- Sugar, 2 tablespoons
- Water, 3 tablespoons
- Heavy cream, 100 ml
- Sugar, 60 g
- Gelatin, 1 ½ tablespoon

Method:

Combine gelatin with water and let it sit for 10 minutes.

Meanwhile combine 60 g sugar and coffee until the sugar dissolves. Now add this mixture to gelatin and stir to melt the gelatin. Keep aside to cool.

Once the mixture has cooled completely transfer to a shallow pan and refrigerate for five hours or until it sets.

Now combine cream with remaining sugar and whip until it thickens slightly.

When the jelly sets completely cut into cubes and arrange in individual serving bowls.

Top with dollops of whipped cream and serve.

8. Japanese Candied Sweet Potatoes

Also known as daigaku-imo in Japanese, candied potatoes are a popular dessert around Japan. The best part about candied potatoes is that is easy and requires less work. While your potatoes are frying you can prepare the sauce and in matter of 15-20 minutes a delicious dessert is ready.

Servings: 2

Preparation time: 20 minutes

Ingredients:

- Sweet potato, 280 g
- Water, 1 teaspoon
- Salad oil, 2 tablespoons
- Black sesame seeds, a handful
- Soy sauce, ½ teaspoon
- Sugar, 2 tablespoons
- Honey, to taste

Method:

Cut potatoes diagonally.

Heat salad oil in a pan and cook potatoes for about 10 minutes.

Meanwhile combine water, soy sauce and sugar in another pan. Boil.

Pour the mixture over potatoes and mix. Dust sesame seeds over it and mix again.

Transfer to serving platter and drizzle honey on top.

9. Matcha Ganache

Matcha powder has a strong and bitter taste to it which when combined with white chocolate bring out a delicate pool of decadent flavors. Wrapping the ganache mixture with plastic makes it easier to take it out once it sets. If you do not wrap it with plastic then be careful when you slice the ganache so you don't break it.

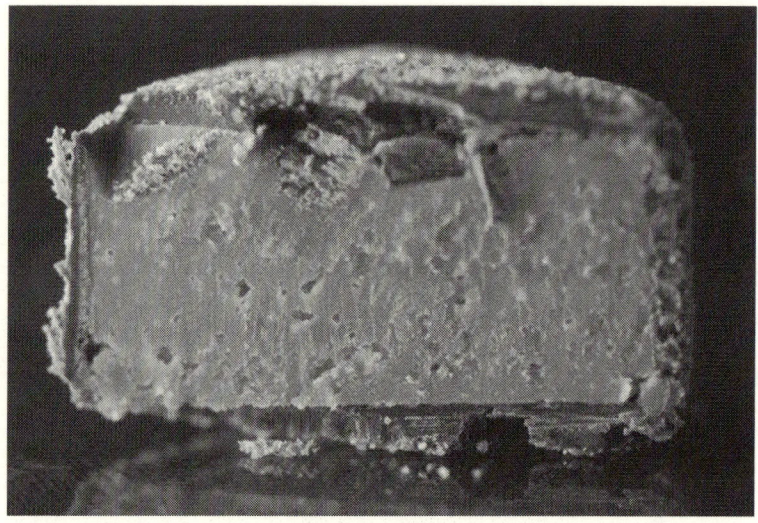

Servings: 4

Preparation time: 20 minutes

Ingredients:

- White chocolate, 100 g
- Butter, 30 g
- Matcha powder, 2 teaspoons
- Fresh cream, 30 g
- Matcha powder, for coating

Method:

Heat cream on low heat and add butter.

Sift matcha powder and add to the heating cream. Combine until butter melts and everything incorporates well.

Meanwhile chop white chocolate into small pieces and add to the cream mixture. Cook until chocolate melts.

Lay plastic over a container and add mixture. Refrigerate for 2.5 hours.

Once the ganache is set slice into small cubes and dust some matcha powder on top.

10. Kabocha Squash Yokan

Sweetened squash is a perfect dessert when you are looking for something sweet and healthy that does not take too long to prepare. You can adjust the sweetness according to your liking. This recipe will make a lot of yokan so refrigerate the leftover in an air tight container.

Servings: 4

Preparation time: 25 minutes

Ingredients:

- Kabocha squash, 500 g
- Salt, 1/5 teaspoon
- Sugar, 80 g
- Water, 50 ml
- Gelatin powder, 5 g

Method:

Peel and slice squash into cubes.

Add to boiling water and boil for 6 minutes.

Transfer squash to a large bowl and mash using a masher.

Now combine salt and sugar with water and heat the mixture in a saucepan. When the particles dissolves completely, stir gelatin and dissolve well.

Stir gelatin in mashed squash and combine well into dough.

Transfer dough to a cling film lined cake pan and even it out. Cover pan with cling film and refrigerate for 5 hours.

11. Mizu Youkan

This version of youkan is made with azuki beans and is perfect for vegetarians. Do not refrigerate youkan for longer period of time only a few hours is enough for it to set. You can also put youkan in different shaped molds for fun shapes.

Servings: 4

Preparation time: 25 minutes

Ingredients:

- Azuki beans, 1 can, boiled
- Water, 300 ml + 300 ml
- Brown sugar, 60 g
- Agar agar powder, 4 g
- Salt, a pinch

Method:

Process beans in 300 ml water until smooth then transfer to a bowl through a sieve.

Heat remaining water in a saucepan and add agar agar. Boil. Now cook on medium heat for 2 minutes while stirring constantly.

Turn off heat and add salt and sugar. Stir well.

Add bean mixture and combine.

Transfer to ramekins and refrigerate for 1.5 hours.

Serve.

12. Fruit Jelly

This beautiful ice cube like jelly dessert is made from fresh fruits and kanten which is a gelatinous substance. The quantity of sugar can always be adjusted according to your liking. For a convenient process use nagashikan for this dessert. Nagashikan is mold that has a removable inner tray and the jelly inside comes out beautifully.

Servings: 9 cubes

Preparation time: 13 minutes

Ingredients:

- Kanten powder, 1 package
- Orange, ½

- Kiwi, 2 pieces
- Blueberries, ¼ cup
- Strawberries, 2, sliced
- Water, 2 cups
- Sugar, 6 tablespoons

Method:

Dissolve kanten in water. Boil. Now turn the heat low and cook for 2 minutes. Whisk occasionally. Turn off heat.

Now add sugar and stir until it dissolves completely.

Transfer a little liquid to a rectangular mold enough that when you arrange fruits on top it won't touch the surface and refrigerate for 10 minutes.

While the mixture is setting in the refrigerator cut fruits into small pieces.

After 10 minutes arrange fruit pieces on top of the mixture and pour the remaining mixture on top. Refrigerate again until the jelly hardens.

Now run a knife through the edges and flip the jelly on counter.

Slice around the fruits into cubes and serve chilled.

13. Castella

Castella also known as kasutera is a traditional Japanese cake made with bread flour, eggs and sugar. The moist and spongy texture of the cake will melt in your mouth while the beautiful brown base looks appealing to the eyes. In case of leftover cake, wrap the slices in plastic and keep at room temperature for not more than two days.

Servings: 6

Preparation time: 50 minutes

Ingredients:

- Bread flour, 1 ½ cup
- Eggs, 7, beaten
- Milk, ¼ cup
- Honey, 1/3 cup
- Sugar, 1 ¼ cup

Method:

Preheat oven to 350 F.

Combine eggs with sugar and beat with an electric beater for 10 minutes.

In another bowl, combine milk with honey then microwave for a few seconds until honey melts.

Meanwhile sift flour in a bowl and keep aside.

Stir half of the honey-milk mixture to the beaten eggs and combine. Now add half of the flour and combine. Repeat with remaining milk and flour. Mix for 3 minutes with a spatula.

Transfer the batter to a lined baking pan.

Bake for 10 minutes then set the temperature to 320 F and bake for another 35 minutes.

Slice it and serve.

14. Dango

These white round morsels are basically dumplings made from tofu and mochiko and are not sweet which is why they are always served with sweet sauces, topping and dipping. In this recipe these chewy balls of goodness are topped with anko.

Servings: 5

Preparation time: 15 minutes

Ingredients:

- Mochiko, 200 g
- Anko
- Tofu, 250 g

Method:

Combine tofu and mochiko in a bowl and form dough.

Take handful of dough at a time in your hands and roll it into round shape. Your dough should not be too loose or firm.

Arrange dough balls on paper towel.

Now boil water in a large pot and carefully add dough balls into boiling water. Cook for 5 minutes then strain them and transfer to paper towel.

Let it cool before serving with anko.

15. Kinako Chestnut

Kinako is roasted soybean flour and is widely used in many Japanese desserts. There are several variations of this recipe. You can make chocolate filling and wrap it around the chestnut jam or make truffles. This is the basic and easiest recipe.

Servings: 3

Preparation time: 15 minutes

Ingredients:

- Chestnut jam, 100 g
- Roasted soybean flour, 4 tablespoons

Method:

In a medium saucepan heat jam and add flour. Stir well to combine.

When everything is well combined, turn off heat and let the mixture cool completely at room temperature.

Now take heaping tablespoons of the mixture and roll it with your hands and form round shaped balls. Repeat with the remaining mixture.

Serve.

16. Matcha Milk Adzuki Bread

These beautiful green colored milk breads are oozing with adzuki beans and are perfect for a warm breakfast. This recipe required a lot of proofing time which can vary according to temperature so make sure you give the dough enough time to rise and take its shape.

Serving: 3

Preparation time: 60 minutes

Ingredients:

- Bread flour, 200 g
- Salt, 1 pinch
- Milk, 110 ml
- Instant dry yeast, 1 teaspoon
- Egg, 1
- Boiled adzuki beans, 80 g
- Sugar, 2 tablespoons
- Matcha, 2 teaspoons
- Skim milk powder, 3 tablespoons
- Unsalted butter, 30 g, at room temperature

Method:

Beat egg and reserve a tablespoon of beaten egg and keep it aside to use in the recipe later.

Microwave milk until heated but not reaching boiling point.

Combine flour with sugar, matcha, skim milk powder and salt in a bowl. Mix well then add yeast.

Stir milk and egg mixture and combine well.

Now add butter and beat using an electric beater.

Put the mixture on a work space and knead using both hands and form dough. Kneading may require around 10 minutes or until the consistency is no more sticky and is like elastic.

Place dough in a bowl and wrap it with plastic. Keep aside for an hour so that it rises well.

When the dough is ready to use, remove plastic wrap and push the dough in the middle with one finger. It should not spring back.

Take out the dough from the bowl and roll it to form a firm ball. Keep it on the plastic and wrap it again. Keep aside for 10 minutes.

Use a bench scraper to make eight portions of dough and roll each portion into flat rectangles.

Now put adzuki beans on it and seal the edges. Carefully lift both ends and twist and link the ends together. Repeat with the remaining seven portions.

Arrange them parchment lined baking sheet and keep aside covered in moistened tea towel for 30 minutes. Make sure you keep them in a warm place this time.

Lastly brush the reserved egg mixture on top of each piece then place the tray in the oven and bake for 15 minutes or until they turn golden brown.

Let it cool before serving.

17. Suama

Suama is a traditional Japanese dessert which is also called celebratory rice cake in English. Red color is used as a symbol to represent the culture of Japan. The ingredients used are rice flour and sugar. For a slight variation and a little drift from the conventional look you can shape suama into any shape you like.

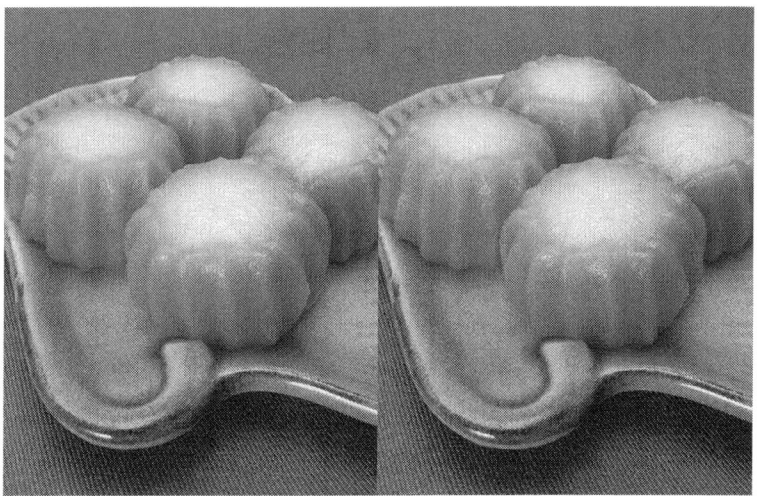

Servings: 3

Preparation time: 20 minutes

Ingredients:

- Joshinko (rice flour), 100 g
- Water, 150 ml
- Red food color, 1 dash
- Sugar, 90 g

Method:

Dissolve food color in little water and mix using a toothpick.

Combine joshinko with sugar and red color mixture and incorporate everything well.

Stir water and mix constantly. Wrap the bowl with plastic and microwave for 3 minutes.

Remove plastic and mix the mixture using chopsticks and cover it again. Microwave for another 2 minutes.

Now transfer the dough to a kitchen towel and wrap it. Knead the dough and make a log. Remove the log from towel and wrap it with plastic and then with sushi rolling mat and secure with a rubber band. This will give suama a firm shape. Keep aside to set for an hour.

Remove the wraps and slice it.

Serve.

18. Taiyaki

Taiyaki is a beautiful cake shaped like a royal fish. Yes, you need a special taiyaki maker for this and these are easily available in the market. This recipe makes five servings of taiyaki that are filled with anko. You can also replace the anko filling with your favorite chocolate spread but that version will not count as authentic Japanese dessert.

Servings: 5 pieces

Preparation time: 25 minutes

Ingredients:

- Cake flour, 1 ¼ cup

- Milk, ¾ cup
- Vegetable oil, 1 tablespoon
- Baking soda, 1 teaspoon
- Egg, 1, beaten
- Baking powder, 1 teaspoon
- Granulated sugar, 3 tablespoons
- Anko (red bean paste), 5 tablespoons

Method:

In a large bowl sift flour, baking powder and soda.

Add sugar and combine.

Whish beaten egg with milk and pour the mixture in the dry mixture bowl. Whisk well. Refrigerate the batter for an hour.

Check the quantity of your batter; it should not be more than 1 ¼ cup.

Now brush taiyaki pan with vegetable oil and pour the 60 % of the mixture into the sections. Place anko in the center and pour remaining batter over it to cover anko.

Cook each side for 3 minutes. When taiyaki picks a nice golden color, remove it from the pan and let it cool on the rack.

Serve.

19. Yatsuhashi

Yatsuhashi means eight bridges in English and has two versions; soft and hard. This recipe makes the soft version filled in tsubuan and shaped into beautiful triangles that are scented with cinnamon. In case you don't have joushinko then increase the quantity of mochiko to 100 g.

Servings: a dozen

Preparation time: 25 minutes

Ingredients:

- Mochiko, 60 g
- Ground cinnamon, 1 teaspoon
- Joushinko, 40 g
- Raw cane sugar, 60 g
- Water, as required
- Ground toasted soybeans, 3 tablespoons
- Tsubuan (sweet adzuki bean paste), 4 tablespoons, for filling
- Ground cinnamon, 1 tablespoon + extra for dusting

Method:

Combine mochiko with 1 teaspoon cinnamon, joushinko and sugar. Add water and whisk well.

Microwave the batter for a minute and mix again using chopsticks.

Now microwave it again for 2 minutes and mix again.

Transfer the dough on a plastic piece and wrap it. Knead the dough carefully with light hands. Knead until the dough is smooth. This may take 10 minutes and you might have to un-wrap the plastic to roll the dough together and wrap it again and knead.

When the dough is ready, mix soybean with remaining cinnamon and dust it over your counter. Place the dough on the counter and roll it flat.

Now cut around 12 to 15 squares from the dough and add ½ teaspoon of tsubuan in the center of each square and fold it into a triangle. Arrange on a tray and dust with remaining soybean and cinnamon mix.

Serve.

20. Kuzumochi

What better can you do with a kuzdu plant other than making a sweet kuzumochi dessert? This white mocha dessert is has plenty of topping options that you can enjoy for example, fruits and their preservatives, condensed milk, molasses and kinako.

Servings: 5

Preparation time: 20 minutes

Ingredients:

- Kuzu powder, 3 ½ oz.
- White sugar, 1 ¾ oz.
- Water, 2 ½ cups + 2 tablespoons

Method:

Combine all the ingredients in a pan and stir well on low heat.

The mixture will change its color and form from opaque white liquid to translucent thick dough like mixture.

Wet the bottom of a medium sized container and transfer the mixture into it. Use a spatula to even it from top.

Let the mixture sit at room temperature for 15 minutes then refrigerate it for an hour and half.

When it is cooled completely, take it out on your kitchen counter and slice it into medium size cubes.

Top with black sugar syrup and toasted and ground soybean powder.

Serve.

21. Manju

Manju is crispy dumpling that comes with a lot of filling options like custard, apple pie, coconut etc. If you have time then let the dough sit in the refrigerator overnight. You can also drizzle you favorite chocolate syrup on top.

Servings: 16 pieces

Preparation time: 30 minutes

Ingredients:

- All-purpose flour, 2 ¾ cup
- Egg yolks, 4
- Granulated sugar, 2 tablespoons
- Unsalted butter, 3 sticks, very cold
- Whole milk, 5 tablespoons
- Salt, ½ teaspoon

For Egg Wash:

- Egg, 1
- Salt, a pinch
- Water, 2 tablespoons
- Filling:
- Apple pie filling, 2 cups

Method:

Combine the dry ingredients together.

Chop solid cold butter and add to the dry mixture. Combine well until it looks like coarse sand.

Whisk milk and yolks in another bowl and pour it in the dry mixture. Whisk well to incorporate.

Now knead the mixture to form smooth dough then wrap it with plastic and keep in the refrigerator for 1 hour.

Once the dough is cooled and set make sixteen portions out of it. Roll each portion flat into a round shape and add a tablespoon of apple pie filling in the center. Pinch the edges together and make a nice round shape.

Arrange on a parchment lined baking tray and brush with egg wash.

Bake for 25 minutes in a preheated oven at 350 F.

Serve when cooled completely.

22. Coconut Pearl Tapioca with Tropical Fruit

This dessert is ideal to serve with tropical fruits and with summers just around the corner you can use any of your favorite fruit as a topping. If you don't have maple syrup then use honey instead or omit both of them completely.

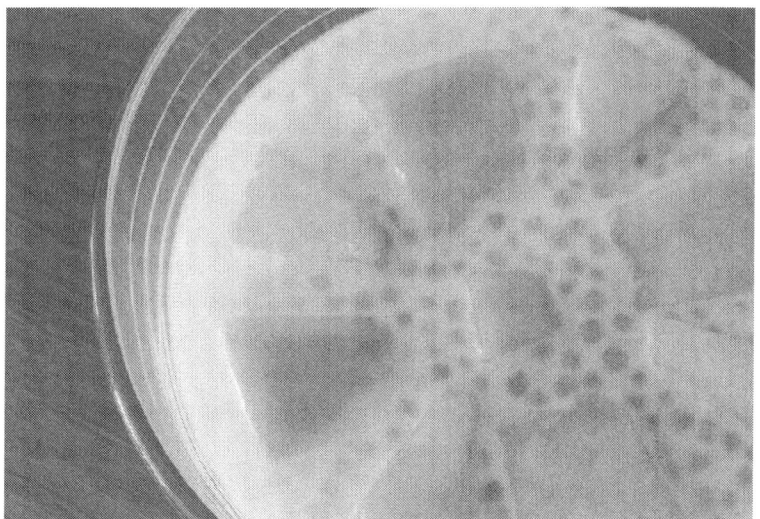

Servings: 4

Preparation time: 30 minutes

Ingredients:

- Coconut milk, 1 can
- Pearl tapioca, ½ cup
- Vanilla extract, 2 teaspoons
- Water, 3 cups
- Granulated sugar, ½ cup
- Salt, 1 pinch
- Lychee, 1 cup, diced
- Pineapple, 1 cup, cubes

Method:

Combine tapioca with sugar, salt and vanilla. Add 2 cups of water and bring the mixture to a boil.

Now turn heat low and simmer for 20 minutes or until the mixture turns translucent. Stir a few times in between.

Add more water if required as the tapioca should not be too chewy.

Stir coconut milk and mix. Let the mixture cool completely.

Transfer to individual serving cups and top with lychee and pineapples. Drizzle maple syrup on top.

23. Japanese Jersey Milk Vanilla Ice-Cream

This recipe makes the creamiest vanilla ice cream of all time. The directions are so easy to follow and require only a handful of ingredients. The flavor of vanilla is not too strong and the texture is perfect. It is a total gourmet experience.

Servings: 2 liters

Preparation time: 20 minutes

Ingredients:

- Jersey cream, 3 cups
- Granulated sugar, 150 g
- Salt, a pinch
- Egg yolks, 3
- Full jersey milk, 3 cups
- Vanilla pod, 1, split
- Pure vanilla extract, ½ teaspoon

Method:

Combine milk with sugar and salt. Add split bean and the seeds inside. Cook in a double boiler for 10 minutes or until the mixture thickens. Discard the pod.

Reduce heat so that water in the bottom section of the boiler comes to a simmer.

Meanwhile beat yolks and add it to the milk. Stir constantly until the mixture picks custard like consistency.

Remove from heat and let it cool.

Now add vanilla extract and cream. Transfer to ice cream maker and follow the instructions.

Serve when chilled and set.

24. Mochi Biscuits

These round biscuits are filled with mocha which you can taste in every single bite. This recipe makes a lot of biscuits so feel free to send some over to friends or pack for kid's lunch. For a small batch you can cut the quantity of ingredients in half.

Servings: 2 dozen

Preparation time: 50 minutes

Ingredients:

- Mochiko flour, 1 box
- Coconut milk, 14 oz.
- Sugar, 1 ½ - 2 cups
- Vanilla extract, 1 teaspoon
- Butter, 2 sticks, softened
- Evaporated milk, 12 oz.

Method:

Preheat oven to 350 F.

Combine all the ingredients together in a large bowl and form a thick batter.

Grease a muffin tray with cooking spray.

Fill each section with 1/3 of the batter.

Pop the tray in the oven and bake for 40 minutes.

Let the biscuits cool for a before popping them out of the pan.

Cool them completely before serving.

25. Karukan

Karukan is a famous Japanese confection made from rice flour and yam potato. The best part about this cake is that it is a no bake cake and it only requires steaming. This cake is also free from those conventional ingredients that every cake recipe has for example, eggs, milk and butter.

Servings: 4

Preparation time: 30 minutes

Ingredients:

- Joshinko (white rice powder), 1 ½ cup
- Yam potato, 24 g
- Water, 100-120 ml
- Sugar, ½ cup

Method:

Peel and dice potato then blend it until smooth.

Add water and sugar and combine well.

Now add rice powder and mix well.

Transfer dough in a baking sheet of a steam basket and steam for 20 minutes on HIGH.

Let the cake cool a little before slicing.

Enjoy.

26. Kabocha Manju

As discussed earlier manju comes with plenty of filling options and this recipe is another version of manju filled with kabocha which is from the family of squash and is also known as Japanese pumpkin in many countries.

Servings: 3

Preparation time: 30 minutes

Ingredients:

- All-purpose flour, 1 ½ cups
- Salt, a pinch
- Baking powder, 1 teaspoon
- Pink color, a few drops

- Sugar, 3 tablespoons
- Water, as required
- Vanilla extract, a few drops
- For filling:
- Kabocha/butternut squash, 2 cups, chopped
- Sugar, ¼ cup

Method:

Boil kabocha in little water until soft. Strain and mash using a masher.

Add sugar to the mashed kabocha and transfer it to a pan. Turn the heat medium-low and cook until the water evaporates completely. Turn off heat and keep aside.

Now to make dough combine all the ingredients together in a large bowl and knead to form a smooth texture.

Divide the dough into three parts and roll each part into a smooth round shape then roll it flat on the counter. Place a heaping tablespoon of filling in the center of the flat disc and seal the edges. Repeat with the remaining two balls.

Prepare the steamer and steam them for 15 minutes.

Serve when cooled completely.

27. Candied Black Beans

Also known as amanatto in Japanese, these candied beans are generously coated in sugar and sweet syrup. The trick to make perfect candied beans is to do the entire cooking on low heat. Increasing the heat even a little towards medium can overcook the beans or the sugar syrup. Store the leftover beans in an air tight jar.

Servings: 1 batch

Preparation time: 1 hour

Ingredients:

- Black beans, 1 lb.
- Granulated sugar, 4 ½ cups
- Superfine sugar, 2 cups
- Baking soda, 1 pinch
- Water, to soak and cook beans
- Salt, 1 teaspoon
- Water, 3 cups

Method:

Rinse beans and discard any stones or irregular beans then soak in plenty of water and keep it overnight.

Next day rinse beans under cold running water. Check again for any irregular beans or stones.

Fill a large pot with water and add beans and baking soda. Simmer on low heat for an hour. Drain and then rinse under cold running water.

To make syrup, combine water with salt and granulated sugar and simmer on low heat for 20 minutes. The syrup with pick a thick consistency and a dark color.

Meanwhile pick any beans that are out from their shells.

Now transfer the beans to the syrup and simmer on low heat for 1 ½ hours.

Turn off heat and let beans sit for 10 minutes before draining them again.

Put sugar in a bowl and toss beans in the sugar and then shift them to a cookie sheet. You may have to work in batches.

Preheat the oven to 175 F and put the cookie sheet in the oven for 5 minutes.

Take them out after 5 minutes and toss them gently and put them again in the oven for 5 minutes.

Turn off the oven but let the beans sit in it for another 5 minutes.

Let the beans cool completely before munching on them.

28. Matcha Green Tea Chia Pudding

This bright green colored pudding is made with matcha powder and chia seeds. Chia seeds a little time to absorb the milk mixture therefore it is best to refrigerate the pudding overnight. You can also substitute maple syrup with agave nectar.

Servings: 2

Preparation time: 15 minutes

Ingredients:

- Blueberries, 1 cup
- Matcha powder, 1 teaspoon
- Almond milk, 2 cups
- Raspberries, 1 cup
- Vanilla extract, 1 teaspoon
- Maple syrup, 2 tablespoons
- Chia seeds, 6 tablespoons

Method:

Combine milk, maple syrup, matcha and vanilla together and process in a blender until smooth.

Put chia seeds in a serving bowl and add matcha-milk mixture over it. Stir for 5 minutes then keep aside for 15 minutes while stirring a few times in between. Let the pudding sit for an hour or two.

Before serving stir again and top with berries.

29. Mochi Ice Cream

Mochi ice cream is widely available across the world in all Japanese restaurants. Your favorite ice cream is wrapped with a delicate shell made of rice flour also known as mochi. The best part about this recipe is that you can use as many flavors of ice creams with a simple mochi base.

Servings: 12 pieces

Preparation time: 33 minutes

Ingredients:

- Shiratamako, ¾ cup
- Potato starch, ½ cup
- Water, ¾ cup
- Sugar, ¼ cup
- Ice cream of your choice

Method:

Line a muffin tray with silicone cupcake liners and scoop out ice cream with a cookie scoop into each section. Freeze the tray until you make mochi and the ice cream is solid.

To make mochi, combine rice flour with sugar. Add water and whisk until a smooth batter forms.

Loosely wrap the bowl with plastic and microwave for a minute. Remove plastic and whisk the batter to combine using a spatula. Put the plastic back on and microwave for another minute. Remove plastic and mix then put the plastic back and microwave for 30 seconds. At this point the batter should turn translucent.

Line parchment paper on work area and dust it with starch. Put mochi mixture on it and dust some more starch on top. Roll the dough flat using a rolling pin.

Transfer mochi along with parchment paper to a baking sheet and put it in the refrigerator for 20 minutes.

Now use a cookie cutter and make around 12 round pieces.

Spread plastic over a plate and start placing each mochi piece on it and wrapping it with plastic. Repeat layering with remaining mochi pieces.

Take each mochi wrapper and place ice cream in between. Enclose the corners and twist the tip a little then wrap in the same plastic. Repeat with remaining balls.

Keep them back in the muffin tray and freeze.

At the time of serving, remove each mochi from plastic then serve.

30. Strawberry Condensed Milk Japanese Shaved Ice

Also known as kakigori in Japanese, this shaved ice dessert is the best way to beat the heat. The flavors of this dessert can vary according to your choice. The most popular ones are lemon, green tea and cherry. The method to make each flavor is exactly the same and taste is mind-blowing.

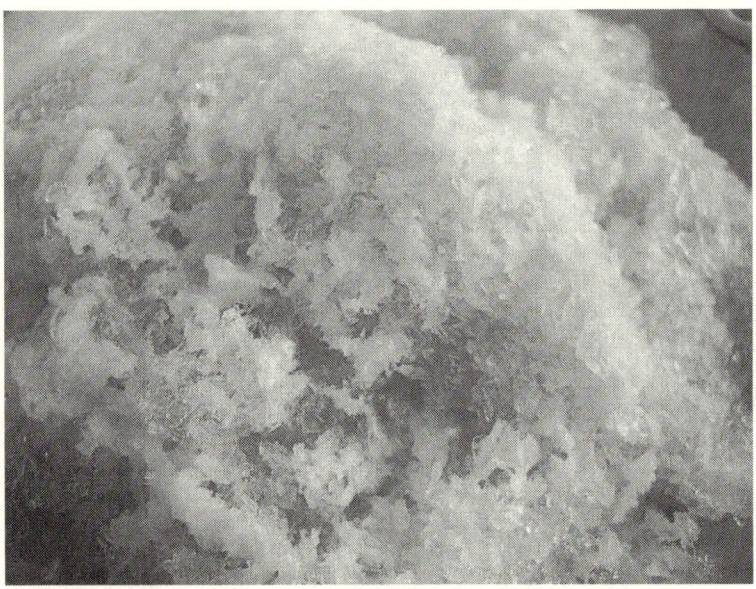

Servings: 3

Preparation time: 45 minutes

Ingredients:

- Strawberries, 1 pound, chopped into large pieces
- Water, 2 cups
- Shaved ice, as required
- Granulated sugar, 2 1/3 cups
- Sweetened condensed milk, 1 can

Method:

To make strawberry syrup, combine sugar and water in a large saucepan and dissolve sugar over medium heat.

Now add strawberries and turn the heat medium-low. Simmer for 10 minutes. Taste the syrup and adjust accordingly.

In a medium bowl strain the strawberries from the syrup then store both syrup and strawberries in different jars in the refrigerator.

When the syrup and stewed strawberries cools, fill individual serving glasses with shaved ice and top it with syrup and spoonful of stewed strawberries followed by swirls of condensed milk.

Serve.

Conclusion

Whether you have recently visited Japan or are planning a visit in near future, there is no way you can resist the temptation of Japanese food, especially desserts. Japan is famous for its mouthwatering cuisine and unique innovations when it comes to the line of desserts.

It was in late 1860's when sugar was easily available across Japan and from that time onwards Japan has always fascinated us with some amazing desserts that took Japanese cuisine to whole new dimensions, depicting that Japanese food is a symbol of simplicity yet versatility.

The Japanese desserts cookbook is all about taking dessert making to the next level. These thirty recipes will give you a decadent experience of a lifetime. Each of these recipes has extraordinary flavor to offer and by the time you will finish experimenting the last recipe of this cookbook you will become an expert chef for Japanese confections.

Japanese desserts are known for their simplicity and delicacy. It's amazing how something so delicious and exquisite can be made from the simplest of ingredients like rice flour and sweet beans. A little bit of color and a few moldings and techniques can execute the finest desserts from your very own kitchen.

These Japanese desserts recipes are designed to make your cooking experience easy and fun. You don't have to be a professional chef to try these out and with a little effort from your end you will be able to make desserts that are one of a kind. These recipes guarantee you perfect taste but you have to do something extra to gain full points on the presentation part.

About the Author

Martha is a chef and a cookbook author. She has had a love of all things culinary since she was old enough to help in the kitchen, and hasn't wanted to leave the kitchen since. She was born and raised in Illinois, and grew up on a farm, where she acquired her love for fresh, delicious foods. She learned many of her culinary abilities from her mother; most importantly, the need to cook with fresh, homegrown ingredients if at all possible, and how to create an amazing recipe that everyone wants. This gave her the perfect way to share her skill with the world; writing cookbooks to spread the message that fresh, healthy food really can, and does, taste delicious. Now that she is a mother, it is more important than ever to make sure that healthy food is available to the next generation. She hopes to become a household name in cookbooks for her delicious recipes, and healthy outlook.

Martha is now living in California with her high school sweetheart, and now husband, John, as well as their infant daughter Isabel, and two dogs; Daisy and Sandy. She is a stay at home mom, who is very much looking forward to expanding their family in the next few years to give their daughter some siblings. She enjoys cooking with, and for, her family and friends, and is waiting impatiently for the day she can start cooking with her daughter.

For a complete list of my published books, please, visit my Author's Page...

https://www.amazon.com/author/martha-stephenson

Author's Afterthoughts

Thanks ever so much to each of my cherished readers for investing the time to read this book!

I know you could have picked from many other books but you chose this one. So a big thanks for downloading this book and reading all the way to the end.

If you enjoyed this book or received value from it, I'd like to ask you for a favor. Please take a few minutes to post an honest and heartfelt review on *Amazon.com*. Your support does make a difference and helps to benefit other people.

Thanks!

Martha Stephenson

Made in the USA
Lexington, KY
29 April 2017